The Kahlil Gibran Diary for 1983

THE KAHLIL GIBRAN
DIARY FOR 1983

ALFRED A. KNOPF

NEW YORK

This diary belongs to

_____

JANUARY

Mon	Tue	Wed	Thu	Fri	Sat	Sun
					1	2
3	4	5	6	7	8	9
10	11	12	13	14	15	16
17	18	19	20	21	22	23
24	25	26	27	28	29	30
31						

MAY

Mon	Tue	Wed	Thu	Fri	Sat	Sun
						1
2	3	4	5	6	7	8
9	10	11	12	13	14	15
16	17	18	19	20	21	22
23	24	25	26	27	28	29
30	31					

FEBRUARY

Mon	Tue	Wed	Thu	Fri	Sat	Sun
	1	2	3	4	5	6
7	8	9	10	11	12	13
14	15	16	17	18	19	20
21	22	23	24	25	26	27
28						

JUNE

Mon	Tue	Wed	Thu	Fri	Sat	Sun
		1	2	3	4	5
6	7	8	9	10	11	12
13	14	15	16	17	18	19
20	21	22	23	24	25	26
27	28	29	30			

MARCH

Mon	Tue	Wed	Thu	Fri	Sat	Sun
	1	2	3	4	5	6
7	8	9	10	11	12	13
14	15	16	17	18	19	20
21	22	23	24	25	26	27
28	29	30	31			

JULY

Mon	Tue	Wed	Thu	Fri	Sat	Sun
				1	2	3
4	5	6	7	8	9	10
11	12	13	14	15	16	17
18	19	20	21	22	23	24
25	26	27	28	29	30	31

APRIL

Mon	Tue	Wed	Thu	Fri	Sat	Sun
				1	2	3
4	5	6	7	8	9	10
11	12	13	14	15	16	17
18	19	20	21	22	23	24
25	26	27	28	29	30	

AUGUST

Mon	Tue	Wed	Thu	Fri	Sat	Sun
1	2	3	4	5	6	7
8	9	10	11	12	13	14
15	16	17	18	19	20	21
22	23	24	25	26	27	28
29	30	31				

SEPTEMBER

Mon	Tue	Wed	Thu	Fri	Sat	Sun
			1	2	3	4
5	6	7	8	9	10	11
12	13	14	15	16	17	18
19	20	21	22	23	24	25
26	27	28	29	30		

OCTOBER

Mon	Tue	Wed	Thu	Fri	Sat	Sun
					1	2
3	4	5	6	7	8	9
10	11	12	13	14	15	16
17	18	19	20	21	22	23
24	25	26	27	28	29	30
31						

NOVEMBER

Mon	Tue	Wed	Thu	Fri	Sat	Sun
	1	2	3	4	5	6
7	8	9	10	11	12	13
14	15	16	17	18	19	20
21	22	23	24	25	26	27
28	29	30				

DECEMBER

Mon	Tue	Wed	Thu	Fri	Sat	Sun
			1	2	3	4
5	6	7	8	9	10	11
12	13	14	15	16	17	18
19	20	21	22	23	24	25
26	27	28	29	30	31	

New Year's Day: January 1st

Kahlil Gibran's Birthday: January 6th (1883)

Lincoln's Birthday: February 12th

St. Valentine's Day: February 14th

Ash Wednesday: February 16th

Washington's Birthday: February 21st

St. Patrick's Day: March 17th

Palm Sunday: March 27th

Passover: March 29th

Good Friday: April 1st

Easter Sunday: April 3rd

Mother's Day: May 8th

Memorial Day: May 30th

Father's Day: June 19th

Independence Day: July 4th

Labor Day: September 5th

Rosh Hashanah: September 8th

Yom Kippur: September 17th

Columbus Day: October 10th

Halloween: October 31st

Election Day: November 8th

Veterans Day: November 11th

Thanksgiving Day: November 24th

Chanukah: December 1st

Christmas Day: December 25th

✦{ *The Present Need* }✦

Be not heedful of the morrow, but rather gaze upon today,
for sufficient for today is the miracle thereof.

Be not overmindful of yourself when you give but be
mindful of the necessity. For every giver himself receives
from the Father, and that much more abundantly.

The week of December 27th to January 2nd

Monday

Tuesday

Wednesday

The week of December 27th to January 2nd

Thursday

Friday

The week of December 27th *to* January 2nd

Saturday

Sunday

The Other Person

Your most radiant garment is of the other person's weaving;
Your most savory meal is that which you eat at the other person's table;
Your most comfortable bed is in the other person's house.

Now tell me, how can you separate yourself from the other person?

The week of January 3rd to January 9th

Monday

Tuesday

Wednesday

The week of January 3rd to January 9th

Thursday

Friday

The week of January 3rd *to* January 9th

Saturday

Sunday

The Desire for Happiness

Heaven did not decree that I pass my days crying out in
agony in the night, saying: "When will come the dawn?"
and when the dawn came, asking: "When will end this
day?" It was not decreed that man should be unhappy and
wretched, for in his depths is created the desire for happi-
ness, because in a man's happiness God is glorified.

The week of January 10th to January 16th

Monday

Tuesday

Wednesday

The *week of* January 10th *to* January 16th

Thursday

Friday

The week of January 10th to January 16th

Saturday

Sunday

✤{ *The Music of the Spheres* }✤

My soul counseled me and charged me to listen for voices
    that rise neither from the tongue nor the throat.
Before that day I heard but dully, and naught save clamor
    and loud cries came to my ears;
But now I have learned to listen to silence,
To hear its choirs singing the songs of ages,
Chanting the hymns of space, and disclosing the secrets
    of eternity.

The week of January 17th to January 23rd

Monday

Tuesday

Wednesday

Thursday

Friday

The week of January 17th to January 23rd

Saturday

Sunday

❖{ The Coming of Spring }❖

All things shall melt and turn into songs when Spring comes. Even the stars, the vast snowflakes that fall slowly upon the larger fields, shall melt into singing streams. When the sun of His face shall arise above the wider horizon, then what frozen symmetry would not turn into liquid melody? And who among you would not be the cupbearer to the myrtle and the laurel?

The week of January 24th to January 30th

Monday

Tuesday

Wednesday

The week of January 24th to January 30th

Thursday

Friday

The week of January 24th to January 30th

Saturday

Sunday

✤{ *Trust* }✤

I saw a companionship between man and all creation;
　And flights of birds and butterflies drawing nigh to
him in safety,
　And gazelles flocking to the pool, trusting.

The week of January 31st *to* February 6th

Monday

Tuesday

Wednesday

The *week of* January 31st *to* February 6th

Thursday

Friday

Saturday

Sunday

⸙{ *The Wise Dog* }⸙

One day there passed by a company of cats a wise dog.

And as he came near and saw that they were very intent and heeded him not, he stopped.

Then there arose in the midst of the company a large, grave cat and looked upon them and said, "Brethren, pray ye; and when ye have prayed again and yet again, nothing doubting, verily then it shall rain mice."

And when the dog heard this, he laughed in his heart and turned from them, saying "O blind and foolish cats, has it not been written and have I not known and my fathers before me, that that which raineth for prayer and faith and supplication is not mice but bones."

The week of February 7th to February 13th

Monday

Tuesday

Wednesday

The week of February 7th to February 13th

Thursday

Friday

The week of February 7th *to* February 13th

Saturday

Sunday

The Lost Sheep

And He looked at me and said, "You do not play upon your flute this day. Whence is the sorrow in your eyes?"

And I answered, "A sheep from among my sheep is lost. I have sought her everywhere but I find her not. And I know not what to do."

And He was silent for a moment. Then He smiled upon me and said, "Wait here a while and I will find your sheep." And He walked away and disappeared among the hills.

After an hour He returned, and my sheep was close beside Him. And as He stood before me, the sheep looked up into His face even as I was looking. Then I embraced her in gladness.

And He put His hand upon my shoulder and said, "From this day you shall love this sheep more than any other in your flock, for she was lost and now she is found."

And again I embraced my sheep in gladness, and she came close to me, and I was silent.

But when I raised my head to thank Jesus, He was already walking afar off, and I had not the courage to follow Him.

The week of February 14th to February 20th

Monday

Tuesday

Wednesday

The week of February 14th *to* February 20th

Thursday

Friday

The week of February 14th *to* February 20th

Saturday

Sunday

⊰ *God Within* ⊱

You invoke the unknown,
And the unknown clad with moving mist
Dwells in your own soul.
Yea, in your own soul your Redeemer lies asleep,
And in sleep sees what your waking eye does not see.
And that is the secret of our being.

The week of February 21st to February 27th

Monday

Tuesday

Wednesday

The week of February 21st to February 27th

Thursday

Friday

The week of February 21st to February 27th

Saturday

Sunday

The week of February 28th to March 6th

Monday

Tuesday

Wednesday

The week of February 28th to March 6th

Thursday

Friday

The *week of* February 28th *to* March 6th

Saturday

Sunday

War

One night a feast was held in the palace, and there came a man and prostrated himself before the prince, and all the feasters looked upon him; and they saw that one of his eyes was out and that the empty socket bled. And the prince inquired of him, "What has befallen you?" And the man replied, "O prince, I am by profession a thief, and this night, because there was no moon, I went to rob the money changer's shop, and as I climbed in through the window I made a mistake and entered the weaver's shop, and in the dark I ran into the weaver's loom and my eye was plucked out. And now, O prince, I ask for justice upon the weaver."

Then the prince sent for the weaver and he came, and it was decreed that one of his eyes should be plucked out.

"O prince," said the weaver, "the decree is just. It is right that one of my eyes be taken. And yet, alas! both are necessary to me in order that I may see the two sides of the cloth that I weave. But I have a neighbor, a cobbler, who has also two eyes, and in his trade both eyes are not necessary."

Then the prince sent for the cobbler. And he came. And they took out one of the cobbler's two eyes.

And justice was satisfied.

The week of March 7th *to* March 13th

Monday

Tuesday

Wednesday

Thursday

Friday

The week of March 7th *to* March 13th

Saturday

Sunday

❧ *The Curse* ❧

An old man of the sea once said to me, "It was thirty years ago that a sailor ran away with my daughter. And I cursed them both in my heart, for of all the world I loved but my daughter.

"Not long after that, the sailor youth went down with his ship to the bottom of the sea, and with him my lovely daughter was lost unto me.

"Now, therefore, behold in me the murderer of a youth and a maid. It was my curse that destroyed them. And now on my way to the grave I seek God's forgiveness."

This the old man said. But there was a tone of bragging in his words, and it seems that he is still proud of the power of his curse.

The *week of* March 14th *to* March 20th

The week of **March 14th** *to* **March 20th**

Thursday

Friday

The week of March 14th *to* March 20th

Saturday

Sunday

One may not reach the dawn save by the path of the night.

The week of March 21st to March 27th

Monday

Tuesday

Wednesday

Thursday

Friday

Saturday

Sunday

Tears and Laughter

Upon the bank of the Nile at eventide, a hyena met a crocodile and they stopped and greeted one another.

The hyena spoke and said, "How goes the day with you, sir?"

And the crocodile answered, saying, "It goes badly with me. Sometimes in my pain and sorrow I weep, and then the creatures always say, 'They are but crocodile tears.' And this wounds me beyond all telling."

Then the hyena said, "You speak of your pain and your sorrow, but think of me also for a moment. I gaze at the beauty of the world, its wonders and its miracles, and out of sheer joy I laugh even as the day laughs. And then the people of the jungle say, 'It is but the laughter of a hyena.'"

The *week of* March 28th *to* April 3rd

Monday

Tuesday

Wednesday

The week of March 28th *to* April 3rd

Thursday

Friday

The week of March 28th to April 3rd

Saturday

Sunday

❧ *The Water of Life* ❧

And how else can it be? In grove and in bower when the rain dances in leaves upon the hill; when snow falls, a blessing and a covenant; in the valley when you lead your flocks to the river; in your fields where brooks, like silver streams, join together the green garment; in your gardens when the early dews mirror the heavens; in your meadows when the mist of evening half veils your way—in all these the sea is with you, a witness to your heritage, and a claim upon your love.

The week of April 4th to April 10th

Monday

Tuesday

Wednesday

Thursday

Friday

The week of April 4th *to* April 10th

Saturday

Sunday

The Cry of the Spirit

I say unto you that every day your spirits cry out and in the night do
your hearts in their anguish call for succor. But you do not hearken to
your spirits and your hearts, for a dying man cannot hear the rattle of
death within him; but those who sit by his bed hear. The slaughtered
bird dances his fantastic dance without direction of will and knows not;
but the beholders know. At what hour of the day sigh not your spirits
in agony? Is it in the morning hour, when the love of existence calls
you and tears from off your eyes the veil of sleep and leads you to the
fields as slaves? Is it at noon, when you would sit in the shade of a tree
to protect yourselves against the burning sun, yet cannot? Or at even-
tide, when you return hungry to your dwellings and find naught save
dry bread and clouded water? Or at nightfall, when weariness throws
you upon your stone couch and gives you fretful slumber; when you
close your eyes in sleep only to awake in fright, imagining the voice of
the Shaikh still ringing in your ears? In what season of the year do your
hearts not weep in sorrow? Is it in the spring, when nature puts on her
new garments and you go out to meet her in your tattered raggedness?
Or is it in the summer, when you reap the harvest and gather in the
yield to the threshing floor and fill the bins of your lord and master
with plenty and receive as your reward only straw and tares? Or in the
autumn, when you gather the fruit and press the grapes in the wine-
press and receive naught of it except vinegar and acorns? Or yet in the
winter, when the elements oppress you and the cold drives you into
your snow-covered huts, while you sit within on the hearth crouching
and fearful of the raging storms? This is then your life, my poor
brethren. This is the night drawing over your souls, unfortunate ones.
These are the shadows of your wretchedness and misery. This is the cry
of anguish which I heard arising out of your depths so that I awoke and
rebelled against the monks and their way of life, and stood alone,
complaining in your name and in the name of justice, which suffers
your sufferings.

The week of April 11th *to* April 17th

Monday

Tuesday

Wednesday

The *week of* April 11th *to* April 17th

Thursday

Friday

The week of April 11th to April 17th

Saturday

Sunday

✠{ *Come and Follow Me* }✠

Then He looked into my eyes and gazed into the depths of my heart. And He said, "I have chosen you and your brother, and you must needs come with me. You have labored and you have been heavy-laden. Now I shall give you rest. Take up my yoke and learn of me, for in my heart is peace, and your soul shall find abundance and a home-coming."

When He spoke thus, I and my brother stood up before Him, and I said to Him, "Master, we will follow you to the ends of the earth. And if our burden were as heavy as the mountain we would bear it with you in gladness. And should we fall by the wayside we shall know that we have fallen on the way to Heaven, and we shall be satisfied."

The week of April 18th to April 24th

Monday

Tuesday

Wednesday

The week of April 18th *to* April 24th

Thursday

Friday

The week of April 18th *to* April 24th

Saturday

Sunday

The week of April 25th to May 1st

Monday

Tuesday

Wednesday

The week of April 25th to May 1st

Thursday

Friday

The week of April 25th to May 1st

Saturday

Sunday

❧{ *Love's Secret* }❧

Love triumphs.
The white and green of love beside a lake,
And the proud majesty of love in tower or balcony;
Love in a garden or in the desert untrodden,
Love is our lord and master.
It is not a wanton decay of the flesh,
Nor the crumbling of desire
When desire and self are wrestling;
Nor is it flesh that takes arms against the spirit.
Love rebels not.
It only leaves the trodden way of ancient destinies for the
    sacred grove,
To sing and dance its secret to eternity.

The week of May 2nd to May 8th

Monday

Tuesday

Wednesday

The week of May 2nd to May 8th

Thursday

Friday

The week of May 2nd to May 8th

Saturday

Sunday

✦{ *Death* }✦

Here I am, beautiful Death. Receive my spirit, reality of my dreams and substance of my hopes. Embrace me, beloved of my soul, for you are merciful and will not abandon me here. You are the messenger of the gods. You are the right hand of truth. Leave me not. How long have I sought you without finding, and called upon you and you hearkened not! But now have you heard me, therefore do not meet my love with shunning. Embrace my soul, my beloved Death.

The week of May 9th to May 15th

Monday

Tuesday

Wednesday

The week of May 9th to May 15th

Thursday

Friday

The week of May 9th to May 15th

Saturday

Sunday

◂{ *According to One of the Marys* }▸

"His head was always high, and the flame of God was in His eyes.

"He was often sad, but His sadness was tenderness shown to those in pain, and comradeship given to the lonely.

"When He smiled His smile was as the hunger of those who long after the unknown. It was like the dust of stars falling upon the eyelids of children. And it was like a morsel of bread in the throat.

"He was sad, yet it was a sadness that would rise to the lips and become a smile.

"It was like a golden veil in the forest, when autumn is upon the world. And sometimes it seemed like moonlight upon the shores of the lake.

"He smiled as if His lips would sing at the wedding feast.

"Yet He was sad with the sadness of the wingèd who will not soar above his comrade."

The week of May 16th to May 22nd

Monday

Tuesday

Wednesday

The *week of* May 16th *to* May 22nd

Thursday

Friday

The week of May 16th *to* May 22nd

Saturday

Sunday

Reason and Passion

Your reason and your passion are the rudder and the sails of your seafaring soul.

If either your sails or your rudder be broken, you can but toss and drift, or else be held at a standstill in mid-seas.

For reason, ruling alone, is a force confining; and passion, unattended, is a flame that burns to its own destruction.

Therefore let your soul exalt your reason to the height of passion, that it may sing;

And let it direct your passion with reason, that your passion may live through its own daily resurrection, and like the phoenix rise above its own ashes.

The week of May 23rd *to* May 29th

Monday

Tuesday

Wednesday

The week of May 23rd to May 29th

Thursday

Friday

The week of May 23rd *to* May 29th

Saturday

Sunday

They deem me mad because I will not sell my days for gold;
  And I deem them mad because they think my days
have a price.

The week of May 30th to June 5th

Monday

Tuesday

Wednesday

The week of May 30th *to* June 5th

Thursday

Friday

The week of May 30th to June 5th

Saturday

Sunday

⊰ *Beyond Wisdom and Folly* ⊱

And call none among you foolish, for in truth we are
neither wise nor foolish. We are green leaves upon the
tree of life, and life itself is beyond wisdom, and surely
beyond foolishness.

The week of June 6th *to* June 12th

Monday

Tuesday

Wednesday

The *week of* June 6th *to* June 12th

Thursday

Friday

The week of June 6th *to* June 12th

Saturday

Sunday

The *week of* June 13th *to* June 19th

Monday

Tuesday

Wednesday

The *week of* June 13th *to* June 19th

Thursday

Friday

The week of June 13th *to* June 19th

Saturday

Sunday

⊰ *The Sacred Loom* ⊱

The sacred loom is given you,
And the art to weave the fabric.
The loom and the art shall be yours forevermore,
And yours the dark thread and the light,
And yours the purple and the gold.
Yet you would grudge yourself a raiment.
Your hands have spun man's soul
From living air and fire,
Yet now you would break the thread,
And lend your versèd fingers to an idle eternity.

The week of June 20th to June 26th

Monday

Tuesday

Wednesday

The *week of* June 20th *to* June 26th

Thursday

Friday

The week of June 20th *to* June 26th

Saturday

Sunday

⊰ *The Playground of Life* ⊱

A minute moving among the patterns of Beauty and the dreams of Love is greater and more precious than an age filled with splendor granted by the weak to the strong.

From that minute rises the god-state of man, and in that age it sleeps a deep sleep veiled by a veil of disturbing dreams;

In that minute is the spirit freed from the burdens of men's conflicting laws, and in that age is it prisoned behind walls of neglect and weighted with chains of oppression.

The week of June 27th *to* July 3rd

Monday

Tuesday

Wednesday

The week of June 27th to July 3rd

Thursday

Friday

The week of June 27th *to* July 3rd

Saturday

Sunday

⊹❴ *Nicodemus* ❵⊹

Do you not remember me, Nicodemus, who believed in naught but the laws and decrees and was in continual subjection to observances?

And behold me now, a man who walks with life and laughs with the sun from the first moment it smiles upon the mountain until it yields itself to bed behind the hills.

The week of July 4th *to* July 10th

Monday

Tuesday

Wednesday

The week of July 4th *to* July 10th

Thursday

Friday

The week of July 4th to July 10th

Saturday

Sunday

✤{ *My Friend* }✤

My friend, I am not what I seem. Seeming is but a garment I wear—a care-woven garment that protects me from thy questionings and thee from my negligence.

The "I" in me, my friend, dwells in the house of silence, and therein it shall remain forevermore, unperceived, unapproachable.

I would not have thee believe in what I say nor trust in what I do—for my words are naught but thy own thoughts in sound and my deeds thy own hopes in action.

When thou sayest, "The wind bloweth eastward," I say, "Aye, it doth blow eastward"; for I would not have thee know that my mind doth not dwell upon the wind but upon the sea.

Monday

Tuesday

Wednesday

The week of July 11th to July 17th

Thursday

Friday

Saturday

Sunday

✤❴ *Freedom* ❵✤

You shall be free indeed not when your days are without a care nor your nights without a want and a grief,

But rather when these things girdle your life and yet you rise above them naked and unbound.

And how shall you rise beyond your days and nights unless you break the chains which you at the dawn of your understanding have fastened around your noon hour?

In truth, that which you call freedom is the strongest of these chains, though its links glitter in the sun and dazzle your eyes.

The week of July 18th to July 24th

Monday

Tuesday

Wednesday

The week of July 18th *to* July 24th

Thursday

Friday

The week of July 18th *to* July 24th

Saturday

.

Sunday

Faith is an oasis in the heart which will never be reached
by the caravan of thinking.

The week of July 25th to July 31st

Monday

Tuesday

Wednesday

The week of July 25th *to* July 3 1st

Thursday

.

Friday

The week of July 25th *to* July 31st

Saturday

Sunday

Man Is Born to Bondage

We, upon the heights, in man's sleep dream our dreams.
We urge his days to part from the valley of twilights
And seek their fullness upon the hills.
Our hands direct the tempests that sweep the world
And summon man from sterile peace to fertile strife,
And on to triumph.
In our eyes is the vision that turns man's soul to flame,
And leads him to exalted loneliness and rebellious
    prophecy,
And on to crucifixion.
Man is born to bondage,
And in bondage is his honor and his reward.

The week of August 1st to August 7th

Monday

Tuesday

Wednesday

The *week of* August 1st *to* August 7th

Thursday

Friday

The week of August 1st to August 7th

Saturday

Sunday

⸬{ *The Golden Belt* }⸬

Once upon a day two men who met on the road were walking together toward Salamis, the City of Columns. In mid-afternoon they came to a wide river and there was no bridge to cross it. They must needs swim, or seek another road unknown to them.

And they said to one another, "Let us swim. After all, the river is not so wide." And they threw themselves into the water and swam.

And one of the men, who had always known rivers and the way of rivers, in mid-stream suddenly began to lose himself, and to be carried away by the rushing waters; while the other, who had never swum before, crossed the river straightway and stood upon the farther bank. Then seeing his companion still wrestling with the stream, he threw himself again into the waters and brought him also safely to the shore.

And the man who had been swept away by the current said, "But you told me you could not swim. How then did you cross that river with such assurance?"

And the second man answered, "My friend, do you see this belt which girdles me? It is full of golden coins that I have earned for my wife and my children, a full year's work. It is the weight of this belt of gold that carried me across the river, to my wife and my children. And my wife and my children were upon my shoulders as I swam."

And the two men walked on together toward Salamis.

The week of August 8th to August 14th

Monday

Tuesday

Wednesday

The week of August 8th *to* August 14th

Thursday

Friday

The *week of* August 8th *to* August 14th

Saturday

Sunday

The week of August 15th to August 21st

Monday

Tuesday

Wednesday

Thursday

Friday

The *week of* August 15th *to* August 21st

Saturday

Sunday

❖{ *The Night of Knowledge* }❖

You grow in sleep, and live your fuller life in your dreaming. For all your days are spent in thanksgiving for that which you have received in the stillness of the night.

Oftentimes you think and speak of night as the season of rest, yet in truth night is the season of seeking and finding.

The day gives unto you the power of knowledge and teaches your fingers to become versed in the art of receiving; but it is night that leads you to the treasure house of Life.

The sun teaches to all things that grow their longing for the light; but it is night that raises them to the stars.

The week of August 22nd to August 28th

Monday

Tuesday

Wednesday

The week of August 22nd *to* August 28th

Thursday

Friday

The week of August 22nd to August 28th

Saturday

Sunday

The Old, Old Wine

Once there lived a rich man who was justly proud of his cellar and the wine therein. And there was one jug of ancient vintage kept for some occasion known only to himself.

The governor of the state visited him, and he bethought him and said, "That jug shall not be opened for a mere governor."

And a bishop of the diocese visited him, but he said to himself, "Nay, I will not open that jug. He would not know its value, nor would its aroma reach his nostrils."

The prince of the realm came and supped with him, but he thought, "It is too royal a wine for a mere princeling."

And even on the day when his own nephew was married, he said to himself, "No, not to these guests shall that jug be brought forth."

And the years passed by, and he died, an old man, and he was buried like unto every seed and acorn.

And upon the day that he was buried the ancient jug was brought out together with other jugs of wine, and it was shared by the peasants of the neighborhood. And none knew its great age.

To them, all that is poured into a cup is only wine.

The week of August 29th to September 4th

Monday

Tuesday

Wednesday

The week of August 29th to September 4th

Thursday

Friday

The *week of* August 29th *to* September 4th

Saturday

Sunday

⚜ *I Will Wash Your Feet* ⚜

And He spoke to the keeper of the inn and said, "Bring be a basin and a pitcher full of water, and a towel."

And He looked at us again and said gently, "Cast off your sandals."

We did not understand, but at His command we cast them off.

Then the keeper of the inn brought the basin and the pitcher; and Jesus said, "Now I will wash your feet. For I must needs free your feet from the dust of the ancient road, and give them the freedom of the new way."

The week of September 5th to September 11th

Monday

Tuesday

Wednesday

The week of September 5th *to* September 11th

Thursday

Friday

The week of September 5th *to* September 11th

Saturday

Sunday

✦{ *A Glimpse into the Future* }✦

From beyond the wall of the Present I heard the praises of mankind.

I heard the voices of bells that shook the very air, heralding the commencement of prayer in the sanctuary of Beauty. Bells wrought by strength from the metal of feeling and raised above that holy shrine—the human heart.

The week of September 12th *to* September 18th

Monday

Tuesday

Wednesday

The week of September 12th to September 18th

Thursday

Friday

The *week of* September 12th *to* September 18th

Saturday

Sunday

⚜ *Love* ⚜

When love beckons to you, follow him,
  Though his ways are hard and steep.
  And when his wings enfold you, yield to him,
  Though the sword hidden among his pinions may
wound you.
  And when he speaks to you, believe in him,
  Though his voice may shatter your dreams as the north
wind lays waste the garden.

The week of September 19th to September 25th

Monday

Tuesday

Wednesday

The week of September 19th to September 25th

Thursday

Friday

The week of September 19th to September 25th

Saturday

Sunday

✦{ *Man* }✦

When out of chaos came the earth, and we, sons of the beginning, beheld each other in the lustless light, we breathed the first hushed, tremulous sound that quickened the currents of air and sea.

Then we walked, hand in hand, upon the gray infant world, and out of the echoes of our first drowsy steps time was born—a fourth divinity, that sets his feet upon our footprints, shadowing our thoughts and desires, and seeing only with our eyes.

And unto earth came life, and unto life came the spirit, the winged melody of the universe. And we ruled life and spirit, and none save us knew the measure of the years nor the weight of years' nebulous dreams, till we, at noontide of the seventh eon, gave the sea in marriage to the sun.

And from the inner chamber of their nuptial ecstasy we brought man, a creature who, though yielding and infirm, bears ever the marks of his parentage.

The *week of* September 26th *to* October 2nd

Monday

Tuesday

Wednesday

The week of September 26th *to* October 2nd

Thursday

Friday

The week of September 26th to October 2nd

Saturday

Sunday

Autumn

Let us go to the vineyard, my love, and press the grapes and store the wine thereof in vessels as the spirit stores the wisdom of ages.

Let us gather the fruits and distill from the flowers their fragrance.

Let us return to the dwellings, for the leaves of the trees are become yellow and the winds have scattered them to make of them a burial shroud for flowers that died grieving at summer's passing.

Come, for the birds have taken flight to the seashore, bearing upon their wings the good cheer of the gardens, bequeathing desolation to the jasmine and the myrtle, and the last tears have been shed upon the sod.

The week of October 3rd to October 9th

Monday

Tuesday

Wednesday

The week of October 3rd *to* October 9th

Thursday

Friday

The week of October 3rd *to* October 9th

Saturday

Sunday

✢❴ *The Unheard Song* ❵✢

"And Life is veiled and hidden, even as your greater self
is hidden and veiled. Yet when Life speaks, all the winds
become words; and when she speaks again, the smiles
upon your lips and the tears in your eyes turn also into
words. When she sings, the deaf hear and are held; and
when she comes walking, the sightless behold her and are
amazed and follow her in wonder and astonishment."

   And he ceased from speaking, and a vast silence enfolded
the people, and in the silence there was an unheard song,
and they were comforted of their loneliness and their
aching.

The week of October 10th to October 16th

Monday

Tuesday

Wednesday

The week of October 10th to October 16th

Thursday

Friday

The week of October 10th to October 16th

Saturday

Sunday

Salome to a Woman Friend

He was like poplars shimmering in the sun;
And like a lake among the lonely hills,
Shining in the sun;
And like snow upon the mountain heights,
White, white in the sun.

Yea, He was like unto all these,
And I loved Him.
Yet I feared His presence.
And my feet would not carry my burden of love
That I might girdle His feet with my arms.

The week of October 17th to October 23rd

Monday

Tuesday

Wednesday

The week of October 17th *to* October 23rd

Thursday

Friday

The *week of* October 17th *to* October 23rd

Saturday

Sunday

❈❲ *The Soul* ❳❈

Say not, "I have found the truth," but rather, "I have found a truth."

Say not, "I have found the path of the soul." Say rather, "I have met the soul walking upon my path."

For the soul walks upon all paths.

The soul walks not upon a line, neither does it grow like a reed.

The soul unfolds itself, like a lotus of countless petals.

The week of October 24th to October 30th

Monday

Tuesday

Wednesday

The week of October 24th to October 30th

Thursday

Friday

The week of October 24th to October 30th

Saturday

Sunday

✦{ *Said a Sheet of Snow-white Paper…* }✦

Said a sheet of snow-white paper, "Pure was I created, and pure will I remain forever. I would rather be burnt and turn to white ashes than suffer darkness to touch me or the unclean to come near me."

The ink bottle heard what the paper was saying, and it laughed in its dark heart; but it never dared to approach her. And the multicolored pencils heard her also, and they too never came near her.

And the snow-white sheet of paper did remain pure and chaste forever—pure and chaste—and empty.

Monday

Tuesday

Wednesday

The week of October 31st *to* November 6th

Thursday

Friday

The *week of* October 3 1st *to* November 6th

Saturday

Sunday

The *week of* November 7th *to* November 13th

Monday

Tuesday

Wednesday

The week of November 7th *to* November 13th

Thursday

Friday

The week of November 7th *to* November 13th

You see but your shadow when you turn your back to the sun.

The *week of* November 14th *to* November 20th

Monday

Tuesday

Wednesday

The week of November 14th *to* November 20th

Thursday

Friday

The week of November 14th to November 20th

Saturday

Sunday

❧ The Pomegranates ❧

There was once a man who had many pomegranate trees
in his orchard. And for many an autumn he would put his
pomegranates on silvery trays outside of his dwelling, and
upon the trays he would place signs upon which he him-
self had written, "Take one for aught. You are welcome."

But people passed by and no one took of the fruit.

Then the man bethought him, and one autumn he
placed no pomegranates on silvery trays outside of his
dwelling, but he raised this sign in large lettering: "Here
we have the best pomegranates in the land, but we sell
them for more silver than any other pomegranates."

And now behold, all the men and women of the neigh-
borhood came rushing to buy.

The *week of* November 21st *to* November 27th

Monday

Tuesday

Wednesday

The week of November 21st to November 27th

Thursday

Friday

The *week of* November 21st *to* November 27th

Saturday

Sunday

Mercy

We are all climbing toward the summit of our hearts'
desire. Should the other climber steal your sack and your
purse and wax fat on the one and heavy on the other, you
should pity him;

The climbing will be harder for his flesh, and the burden
will make his way longer.

And should you in your leanness see his flesh puffing
upward, help him a step; it will add to your swiftness.

The week of November 28th to December 4th

Monday

Tuesday

Wednesday

The week of November 28th to December 4th

Thursday

Friday

The week of November 28th to December 4th

Saturday

Sunday

✦{ *The Vine of Man* }✦

We have planted man, our vine, and tilled the soil
In the purple mist of the first dawn.
We watched the lean branches grow,
And through the days of seasonless years
We nursed the infant leaves.
From the angry element we shielded the bud,
And against all dark spirits we guarded the flower.

The week of December 5th to December 11th

Monday

Tuesday

Wednesday

The week of December 5th *to* December 11th

Friday

The week of December 5th *to* December 11th

Saturday

Sunday

⚜ The Holy One ⚜

In every aspect of the day Jesus was aware of the Father.
He beheld Him in the clouds and in the shadows of the
clouds that pass over the earth. He saw the Father's face
reflected in the quiet pools, and the faint print of His feet
upon the sand; and He often closed His eyes to gaze into
the Holy Eyes.

The night spoke to Him with the voice of the Father,
and in solitude He heard the angel of the Lord calling to
Him. And when He stilled Himself to sleep, He heard the
whispering of the heavens in His dreams.

The *week of* December 12th *to* December 18th

Monday

Tuesday

Wednesday

The week of December 12th *to* December 18th

Thursday

Friday

The week of December 12th *to* December 18th

Saturday

Sunday

The week of December 19th to December 25th

Monday

Tuesday

Wednesday

The week of December 19th *to* December 25th

Thursday

Friday

The week of December 19th *to* December 25th

Saturday

Sunday

❧{ *Your Neighbor* }❧

Your neighbor is your other self dwelling behind a wall.
In understanding, all walls shall fall down.

Who knows but that your neighbor is your better self
wearing another body? See that you love him as you
would love yourself.

He too is a manifestation of the Most High, whom you
do not know.

Your neighbor is a field where the springs of your hope
walk in their green garments, and where the winters of
your desire dream of snowy heights.

Your neighbor is a mirror wherein you shall behold
your countenance made beautiful by a joy which you
yourself did not know, and by a sorrow you yourself did
not share.

The week of December 26th *to* January 1st

Monday

Tuesday

Wednesday

The week of December 26th *to* January 1st

Thursday

Friday